Good News! Jesus Is Born!

Retold by
Pat Floyd
Illustrated by
Tom Dunnington

Graded Press

NASHVILLE

Copyright © 1987 by Graded Press
All rights reserved.
ISBN 0-939697-38-6

Manufactured in the United States of America

Long, long ago
people were waiting to hear good news.
They needed to know that God loves everyone.
They needed to stop fighting.
They needed to start loving.
They needed to live as God's children.

A man named Isaiah said, "Good news is coming!
Go up to the mountain top and tell all the people.
'Good news is coming!'"
Isaiah's words are in the Bible.
He also said, "A wonderful child will be born."

Many years later
A woman named Mary heard good news.
An angel told Mary this news:

"God is pleased with you, Mary.
You will have a baby boy.
You will name your baby Jesus.
Jesus will be God's son."

Before Mary's baby was born,
Mary and her husband, Joseph, had to take a trip.
They had to go to Bethlehem.

Bethlehem was far away from their home in Nazareth.
Mary and Joseph walked on long, dusty roads.
Their donkey clip-clopped along with them.
Good news seemed far, far away.

After many days Mary and Joseph came to Bethlehem.
They went to the inn where travelers stayed,
but the inn was full.
They had no place to stay.

Mary and Joseph were tired.
They wondered where they could stay.
The time had come for Mary's baby to be born.
Would good news ever come for them?

The innkeeper let Mary and Joseph
stay in the stable with the animals —
the donkeys and cows and sheep and goats
and the chickens softly clucking.

In that stable Mary's baby was born,
and they named him Jesus.
Mary laid him in a manger
where hay was kept for the animals.
Good news had come in Bethlehem!

The night Jesus was born
shepherds were in the fields
taking care of their sheep.
An angel from God came to the shepherds and said,
"Don't be afraid. I have good news for you.
Today God's son is born in Bethlehem."

Suddenly the sky was full of angels singing, "Glory to God in heaven and peace to those who please God."

When the angels had gone away,
the shepherds said to one another,
"Let us go to Bethlehem.
Let us see what God is telling us."

The shepherds hurried to Bethlehem.
They went to the stable where they saw
Mary and Joseph and the baby,
just as the angels had told them.
Good news had come to the shepherds!

The shepherds returned to their sheep
singing thanks to God
for the good news they had seen and heard.

They told everyone they met about the angels and about the baby Jesus and about the good news of God's love.

A bright star brought good news
to wise men who lived far away.
The bright star meant that a baby had been born.
This baby would be the most important person
in all the world.

The wise men wanted to see the new baby.
They traveled a very long way to find him.
The star showed them the way.

The wise men followed the star all the way
to the place where Jesus was.
There the wise men gave Jesus gifts
and knelt down and worshiped him.
Jesus' birth was good news.

All the people in the world
are waiting to hear good news.
They need to hear about Jesus' birth.
They need to know what Jesus said and did
when he grew up to be a man.
Jesus made sick people well.
He fed hungry people.
He told people to do what is right.
He taught them to pray.
He said, "God loves everyone in the world so much
that God sent me to show God's love."

Go, tell it on the mountain,
Over the hills and everywhere.
Go, tell it on the mountain
That Jesus Christ is born.[1]

Go, tell about the shepherds
Over the hills and everywhere.
Go, tell about the shepherds,
That Jesus Christ is born.

Go, tell about the manger,
Over the hills and everywhere.
Go, tell about the manger,
That Jesus Christ is born.

Go, tell about the baby,
Over the hills and everywhere.
Go, tell about the baby,
That Jesus Christ is born.

[1]Copyright © 1940 by John W. Work.

To Parents and Teachers

These storybooks and cassettes are designed to help children know and love the Bible and live by the Bible's teachings. You can help by reading and listening with children and by encouraging them to read and listen on their own.

You may also wish to read with children some of the Scripture passages on which GOOD NEWS! JESUS IS BORN! is based: Luke 1:26-38 and 2:1-20; Matthew 1:18–2:11; Isaiah 9:6 and 40:9.

Some of the other titles in this series are *Rejoice! Jesus Is Alive!*, *David's Many Ways to Praise*, and *Too Many Brothers: The Story of Joseph*.